yellow-eyed penguin

adelie

African penguin

macaroni penguin

emperor penguins

king penguin

chinstrap penguin

snares penguin

southern rockhopper penguin

little penguin

northern rockhopper penguin

1 They take flying leaps

Penguins are super-speedy swimmers. They dart and dive, using their flippers like underwater wings. This helps them to twist and turn as they swim and search for fish to eat.

gentoo penguins

leopard seal

3 6109 00545 8523

Penguins cannot fly. But they do shoot up and out of the water to escape predators with a burst of speed. They also pop up onto the rocks or ice to rest.

bubbles

silverfish

2 They can see underwater

Penguins can dive deep underwater in their search for fish. Their eyes are a special shape, which helps them see well underwater. They are protected by transparent eyelids.

Galapagos penguins

They can also see squid as they change color, and feast on tiny shrimp-like creatures called krill. But their ocean food is being scooped away by giant floating nets that sometimes tangle penguins too.

SHOW YOU LOVE A PENGUIN

Look up the Good Fish Guide to find fish caught sustainably without hurting other sea life.

marine iguana

sally lightfoot crab

sardines

3 They go tobogganing

Penguins walk with a slow waddle. If they want to speed up on icy ground, they flop onto their tummy and slide. Tobogganing is easy and a lot more fun.

snowy sheathbill

chick

ice

chinstrap penguins

In rocky places, penguins jump to get around.
They slip, tumble, and hop along!

They have salty sneezes

Penguins swallow lots of salty water when they gulp their prey of fish and krill. They have a special gland at the top of their beaks that helps them get rid of excess salt. It dribbles down their beaks and then shoots off like a sneeze when they shake their heads.

rockhopper penguins

albatross

Salt water doesn't quench penguins' thirst. If they want a drink, they sip freshwater from pools and streams or just nibble on snow.

SHOW YOU LOVE A PENGUIN

Discover penguin-friendly power! Oil spills pollute places where penguins live: ask if greener energy is lighting your home.

beak

rocky shore

They cuddle up close together

Most penguins live in cold places. To keep warm, they have thick skin and blubbery fat. Some species of penguins huddle together in big groups, taking turns to shuffle into the warmest spots in the middle of the group.

ice

emperor penguins

But penguins still get chilly feet. They hunch over their feet or rock on their heels to keep them off the ice. Their bare feet help them to walk without slipping, and penguins use them to steer as they swim.

chicks

seal pup

6 They love rocks

When penguins are trying to find a mate, they are elegant and polite. They wave their heads and bow to impress their new partner. They sing and dance to get to know each other and to recognize each other if they have mated before.

nest

rocks

Together, they make some strange nests. Some burrow into their own poop while others put rocks in a pile. These penguins offer pebble gifts to each other as they build their nests.

adelie penguins

egg

7 The dads are the babysitters

Emperor penguins don't build nests. They balance their eggs on their feet instead and keep them warm by tucking them into a snug pouch. The female lays the egg and shuffles it over to the male. If the egg touches the ice, it will freeze.

male penguin

female penguin

Male emperor penguins keep the eggs warm until they hatch, while the females make the long and difficult journey to the sea to find food for themselves and their chicks.

emperor penguins

egg

pouch

SHOW YOU LOVE A PENGUIN

Adopt a penguin through a charity like the WWF! This helps protect the seas where they live.

8 They bare all

Unlike most animals that molt, penguins lose all their feathers at once. During this "catastrophic molt," they are no longer waterproof, so they can't fish!

feathers

macaroni penguins

For two weeks each year, penguins are stuck on land looking very scruffy indeed. When their feathers grow back, they trap warm air next to the penguin's skin. This helps them survive in freezing seas.

SHOW YOU LOVE A PENGUIN

Peek at a penguin! Spy on penguins with live cameras filming 100 locations at Zooniverse Penguin Watch.

crest

molt

9 They march for their babies

Most penguins migrate. They swim, waddle, or toboggan a long way to find food or a place to breed. Emperor penguins make the most spectacular and difficult journey of all.

These penguin giants march in long, wobbly lines for weeks. They are heading for ice cliffs that shelter them from the freezing winds and storms that rage while they lay their eggs.

emperor penguins

10 They have so many friends

Almost all penguins gather in huge, noisy groups called colonies to breed. They are smelly too because there is lots of penguin poop. The area of black stained ice in some colonies is so big that it can be seen from space!

giant petrel

colony

SHOW YOU LOVE A PENGUIN

Find out about climate change in Antarctica! Discover what happens when the ice melts.